BAL ACT

Part One of a
Journal for all Relationships

by • Sally and Vince Huntington

OTHER BOOKS BY THESE AUTHORS

The Huntington Sexual Behavior Scale. Weidner & Sons, New Jersey
ISBN 0-938198-03-3 March 1998

Men & Sex, Heroes & Jerks. Cutler Publishing, La Jolla, California
ISBN 0-938198-03-3 October 2000

Reprisal, a (psychological) novel. (Includes the personality disorders
from the DSM-IV). (Amazon), Charleston, South Carolina
ISBN 1-4196-3134-9 October 2006

———————————

ISBN: 145156287X
ISBN-13: 9781451562873
LCCN: 2010905752

THE
BALANCING
ACT

Part One of a
Journal for all Relationships

The Balancing Act

Me vs. Me
and
She vs. He

HOW TO BALANCE OUT
ANY RELATIONSHIP!

The Balancing Act is published as Part I of
"A Journal for All Relationships"
(In progress)
by Vince and Sally Huntington, © January 2011.
They invite you to count on these books to provide objective
insight to help you improve the quality of *any* relationship.

This no-nonsense book is about how to keep the original electricity of any romance alive by *consciously* undoing some damage that nature plants at the *beginning of any romance, yours* included. This is the stuff they should have taught us early in life, but *they* didn't know its real value then.

This is not one of those "he-said, she-said" books about communication as in those walk-on-eggshell approaches to relationships. When you integrate *these* guides, the quality of your life *will be better* not only in romantic relationships, but in *any* relationship, including the one you have with your local grocer.

BUT FIRST...WHO ARE YOU, ANYWAY?

No matter what took place and caused the birth and presence of you, of me, of any one individual, *that* will <u>never</u> happen again...never...ever. Ask the DNA people. Each of us is one in a million-trillion-zillion, plus or minus. Births continue daily but there will never be another you. You get to go through life individually! No instruction book with rules cut especially for you. Being individuals, though, we are on our own most of the time, and, when alone, we do tend to get lonely. To stop the loneliness, we generally turn to other individuals for relief. However, if we begin to get too much of *them,* we can begin to feel smothered or controlled. We then turn back to ourselves to regain a sense of autonomy until we begin to feel loneliness again, then back to togetherness, back and forth, forth and back. So, in short, it seems we are made up of two basic chunks: (1) separateness and (2) togetherness. This book is about keeping the best balance of those two very different chunks.

Separateness, *individuality, autonomy, self-identity,* and *uniqueness* are some of the words we use to identify ourselves when we talk about that part of us that is separate from all others and from any other. It is the "I" in "Me."

Togetherness*, dependency, closeness, social identity* and *enmeshed* are some of the words used to describe the *opposite side* of separateness, i.e., connectedness. It is the "Me" in "Us." Our overall personalities (and our overall happiness) are made up of the details of how well we balance our *separateness* with our *togetherness.* It's not difficult to stay balanced once you understand the signals of being *out of balance.*

Neither the separateness nor the togetherness (many terms are used interchangeably[1]) can be ignored. Well, actually, we are our own person and we can elect to try to ignore separateness

---

1 <u>Separateness</u>: alone, apart, autonomy, being myself, I, independence, individuality, me, myself, uniqueness.
<u>Togetherness</u>: connected, closeness, dependency, enmeshed, joined at the hip, us, we, being close, social me.

and togetherness, but neither can be ignored for very long at any one time because the results are too alien to our natural needs. For instance, if *autonomy* (our *separateness*) is ignored for very long, we first feel unsettled, *bothered*. If ignored longer, we feel controlled, over monitored. If ignored *too* long, we feel over controlled, even trapped, overwhelmed by the demands of others, and eventually (gasp) smothered. ("Dammit, stop smothering me.")

If *dependency* (our need for *togetherness*) is ignored for very long, we can feel awkward, adrift, and disconnected. If ignored longer, we feel out of touch, perhaps unimportant, and rejected. If ignored for *too* long, we feel alone, lonely, unloved, and, eventually, become deeply sad. ("Come close. I need time with you.")

When anyone says, "I'm just not myself today," it's a wiser saying than we give credit for, because only that person can identify with the "myself" he or she is missing. One problem is, few of us pay real attention to "myself" until something goes astray. There is a human rule of thumb that seems to come into play a lot. As long as things are okay, we are okay. When they are not okay, we blame someone else. It is just what we do. This book is intended to help you be more responsible for making and keeping things okay and for blaming others less and less.

"OKAY" IS BEING BALANCED

To feel "okay," *separateness* and *togetherness* seem to need to be evenly spaced or balanced, not too much of one, nor too much of the other. We cannot tell how much this need for balance between *separate* and *together* comes naturally as a basis of our genetic makeup, like some internal timer is protecting our independence but at the same time is keeping us socialized enough to feel safe, valued, or *loved*. There is plenty of evidence that we might have almost purposefully socialized this *independence* vs. *dependency* into our lives over eons without actually meaning to do so at conscious community levels.

THE BALANCING ACT

This balance phenomenon is fascinating, even eerie at times. Observing the balancing experience in motion exposes all the information we need in order to understand companionship, friends, mutual exchange of caring, and love: the falling-in, falling-out, search-for, fulfillment-by, crushed-by, tricked-by, lost-in, et al. And, you guessed it already, maintaining the best balance *while* we are experiencing love itself *is* what love is all about.

Please be careful at this point, for it is natural for us all to believe we have this balancing down pat if we blindly adhere to all social "rules" we can then assume, or pretend, we are in a balance with life. Watch out. Social rules are not tailored for *individuals*; they are generalized for everyone. Are you the same as everyone?

WATCH THE BALANCE IN ACTION

Autonomy and dependency (auto-dep) are both wonderful. One is who we are when alone; the other is who we are when with someone. However wonderful they are on their own, autonomy and dependency don't mix easily. Each demands full attention at times and, if run to their extremes, expose all the frailties we witness in human interactions. Such as (alphabetically):

abandonment, control, cruelty, denial, desertion, discrimination, fear, force, greediness, guilt, manipulation, patronization, punishment, rejection, sacrifice, seduction, shame, smothering, violation.

Movies, television, poetry, music, almost any daily drama thrives on stories of being out of balance, and we all talk about aspects of it. If anything defines *the meaning of life*, it is learning the signs of, and then openly honoring the balance between, separateness and togetherness. Personal uneasiness happens when this critical equilibrium is ignored, underestimated or otherwise left to accomplish itself. You will likely see yourself in the paragraphs that follow.

WHAT ARE THESE THINGS WE BALANCE?

Autonomy is overall freedom from being controlled, and this includes freedom from those unwanted feelings listed above. Autonomy is the creative "you" that defines you as separate in identity from anyone else in the world. Your autonomy defines your individuality, your personality, and your accomplishments. You are delightful, inquisitive, you make music and art, you appreciate sunsets and beauty, and you design buildings, tunnels, organizations, and businesses. You experience ideas, elation, freedom, satisfaction, pleasure, and the rewards of being pleased with yourself. The *far end of this autonomy*, when deep into your "self," perhaps being *too long* in the extremes or heights of autonomy, suddenly (no matter how wonderful it is/ was a microsecond ago), you may begin to feel alone, disconnected, uneasy, not as good as you were a moment ago. You might begin to feel unwanted, unworthy, unnecessary, rejected, alienated, or even frightened and sad, and, one of the worst feelings we can have, *lonely*. We avoid this feeling of loneliness when we can. Well, we sure *try* to avoid it.

When lonely, we believe if only we had *someone* to be with, the loneliness would end and everything would be all right. From *separateness* to *togetherness*, we go back and forth, forth and back, depending on how lonely we feel when alone and how smothered we feel when together. We recognize *lonely* as the far end or the negative end of autonomy, and *smothered* as the far end or negative end of together.

The extreme ends of either togetherness or autonomy suck!

SMOTHERED TOGETHERNESS ROMANCE BALANCED FULFILLED AUTONOMY LONELY

[--------------------*Feeling Loved*------------]

"Quit smothering me, will you?"
"But I just want time with you."
"Well, I just want to finish this book."
"What's the book about?"
"Oh, nothing. Something I'm interested in, something private."
"Ohhh!"

Togetherness and Autonomy *both* have secret sides and open sides:

TOGETHERNESS < ROMANCE < BALANCED > FULFILLED > AUTONOMY

Private things of ours & Private places I go
Private things of mine & Private things I do
Private things of yours & Private things you do
Open things we do & Open things I do

LEARN FROM THE DOG AND CAT

People who can't handle the autonomy of a cat will likely have trouble managing the *autonomy* of a person. A cat moves in close: "pet me, hold me, ..." then quickly leaves with a tail's up "I've had enough of you" attitude. Similarly, if someone becomes overwhelmed by a dog's dependency ". . . pant, pant, pet me, pet me, pet me. . . " they may well have trouble managing the dependency of a similarly needy person.

WHAT'S LOVE GOT TO DO WITH IT?

For most of us, a gratifying *romantic love* seems to be the positive end of togetherness while *unhindered personal fulfillment* is the positive end of separateness. An overall feeling of *being loved* is the overlapping phenomenon between the two chunks.

This use of the word *love* means both romantic love and social acceptance love; people to talk to, work with, enjoy being around. To feel good about life and about yourself; to be *truly* balanced, you want to feel loved, but still feel free to be *you*.

We humans often put off true separate personal fulfillment until we *accomplish* feeling truly loved simply because life without love, for most, has an ongoing feeling of emptiness, of being incomplete. To delay separate autonomous fulfillment in favor of romantic love is not a wise thing, as you will see later. It distorts autonomy and gives dependency unwarranted power. (Quit smothering me!).

It is not that being *together* or being in love stops personal fulfillment, no. Some of us, in error, permit love to stop autonomy. Though it seems a contradiction, true fulfillment of our autonomous self *seems* only possible when we know we are also in love and *continue to feel loved while out there* exercising our autonomy. In true love we do not (within reason) feel limited by *encumbrances* of being in love.[2] The love has to be of such honest quality that if loneliness seeps into autonomy, it also comes with reminders (recalled from within ourselves) that we are loved, to not panic and run back, abandoning our autonomy.[3] When truly loved, any loneliness is really a reminder of how great it is that *being loved* is present, it's just over there right now, voluntarily. We can turn and be loved when ready, whether off on a six-month tour with the military[4] or a night out shopping or spending time with friends or just pulling back to quietly read a good book.

---

2 *True love* is examined and particularized in detail in *True Love and That Other Kind* (Huntington/Huntington), Part III of this *Journal for All Relationships*.

3 Recalling from within our memories and experiences and *getting an accurate picture* that we can use to serve the current moment is one simplistic definition of mental health, i.e., the basis for the ability to face life calmly. Detailed in *No Anger Beyond This Point* (Part II of this *Journal for All Relationships*, Amazon, © 2011, V. and S. Huntington.

4 The impact of becoming lonely *must* be considered, even tested, when the source of being loved is unavailable or tested too strongly, as in long military deployments or leaving the family to job search or work long periods. Long absence is not a normal state in the balance of autonomy/ dependency, a state we know a lot about. If you notice, bicoastal relationships fit only a few.

BALANCE OF AUTONOMY AND DEPENDENCY

The following description of the conscious process of balancing *togetherness* (dependency*)* with *separateness* (autonomy) is the first of several ways to define the balancing act. Because we now have knowledge that separateness becomes loneliness, we have similar knowledge that togetherness can become smothering.[5] Once we have the feeling of being powerfully and beautifully in love (or socially accepted), we voluntarily set aside parts of the romantic love (or social interaction) in favor of autonomy in order to avoid feeling smothered by the romantic love (or social obligation). To re-remind you, those *who have not mastered the equalizing of autonomy/dependency* often might see love as the beginning of the potential loss of autonomous freedoms.

Now that you are familiar with some of the terms, (autonomy, dependency, togetherness, smothered, abandoned) please take a look at the two simple tests in Appendix I. The test will help you see where your life is or is not currently balanced. Re-test after completing the book and see the insight you've gained.

TO BALANCE IT ALL, BACK AND FORTH, FORTH AND BACK

Of course, to balance it all, one must learn to identify one's own personal experience associated with the extreme feelings of *separateness* (loneliness) and the extremes of *togetherness*

---

5   D. H. Lawrence (1885–1930), "You love me so much, you want to put me in your pocket. And I should die there smothered." *Sons and Lovers,* 1913.

(smothered). Once clear, it is possible to experience your life as these two big easily recognized chunks: separateness and togetherness. Once you identify your needs in these areas, you can manage them into balance. When not balancing yourself, the extremes of loneliness and of being smothered appear to want to *win over* one another again and again. Typical comments that express these *extremes* in action are:

When Really Lonely

"If I just had *someone*, I'd be happy."
"If I had <u>anyone</u>, I'd be happy."
"I'd love *anyone* who could end this loneliness."
"I'm so lonely, I could die."

When Really Smothered

"I can't find *anyone* good enough anymore."[6]
"They're always asking—'where are you going?' "
"I need my space, damn it."
"I just want some alone time."

---

6   Bernard Shaw (1856–1950), *"There are two tragedies in life. One is to <u>not</u> get your heart's desire. The other is to get it."* And Lord Tennyson (1809–1892) agrees: " *(It were) possible, after long grief and pain to find the arms of my true love round me once again"; "[A]nd most of all would I flee from the cruel madness of love."*

WHEN LOOKING FOR THE BALANCE

When love comes along, our *need for romance* or a need to end the loneliness disconnects you (me) from our *autonomous* identity enough to where, at times, we are convinced we only felt nourished by being in love. Autonomy is out this year—togetherness is in.

If you look back to having been in love, *in love* (the enraptured, engulfed, and deliciously satisfying part) seemed to become its own identity. However, what is peculiar is, as rapturous and delicious as any moment of love was at any time, it does seem to go away—eventually—someplace. Why does it go away? Where *does* it go? Why do we even notice that it is gone? What is different with it *gone*? And, why not notice *before* it went away or that it was even going anywhere—until it's too late to stop it from going? "Ahh, sweet mystery of life…"[7]

Actually, even when it seems *gone*, if you recall from within an accurate picture of it as it has served you both, you will see *love is still there*, enmeshed within the *autonomy* and the *togetherness*. When your autonomy screams for recognition, the memory of not being able to live without love will fade into the background, and at this point, often, many of us take that as a sign that love is over.

But it is not; it is simply going to be placed on hold for now.

At a basic level, you (any of us) can be thankfully disconnected from the *lonely side* of autonomy by the *togetherness* of being in love, and we relish those experiences. We can also be thankfully disconnected from the smothering side of togetherness (love) by the rewards of individuality and autonomy; we often simply misread it. Never forget: in autonomy, we meet our own needs; in togetherness, we rely on (ask) someone else to meet our needs. Autonomous happiness is in our own hands; dependent happiness (love and/or social acceptance)

---

7 *"Ahh Sweet Mystery of Life (At Last I've Found You)."* A Victor Herbert operetta (1910) popularized in the film *Naughty Marietta* (MGM), whereby Jeanette MacDonald won her first Oscar in 1935.

is in someone else's hands. The other person will only want to try to meet your needs for love if you meet his or hers. By the way, what are his or her specific needs of love? What are *yours*? Exactly!

By definition, love *cures* loneliness. But that's not all it does. No sir! If left to itself, it would also kill autonomy and engulf all individuality into togetherness.

So, what is love exactly? Is it truly, as said in the movies, "*the morning and the evening star*"?[8]

A THOUSAND THOUSAND SONGS . . . ?

Well, maybe a *few hundred* songs have actually been written which display autonomy and dependency out of balance one way or another. To partially quote a few lines from a few: *By the time I get to Phoenix*[9] The lyrics state: "And she'll cry just to think I'd really leave her, Tho' time and time I try to tell her so, She just didn't know I would really go." We offer they didn't take time to discuss autonomy/togetherness and discover he was being smothered.

In *Don't Fence Me In,*[10] songwriter Cole Porter described a cowboy who knew himself so well he declared openly to one and all, "I want to ride to the ridge where the west commences, Gaze at the moon until I loose my senses, I Can't look at hobbles and I can't stand fences, Don't fence me in."

In the song *Without Your Love*[11], Barbra Streisand sings "I will not leave you . . . I would not be alive today, without your love." When that "someone" reaches to regain autonomy, will the

---

8   From the movie *Elmer Gantry*, 1960, "*Love is the morning and the evening star*" (Richard Brooks, director and screenwriter, from the novel by Sinclair Lewis, 1927). Con man/evangelist Elmer Gantry's all-purpose seduction line used for both individuals and groups. Used here to acknowledge one's own hopeless romanticism and the eternal need to define "what is love."

9   *By the Time I Get to Phoenix* written by Jimmy Webb, 1965.

10 *Don't Fence Me In* written by Cole Porter, 1934.

11 Without Your Love, written by Ashley Gibb, 1975.

singer *really* die? And further - in the song, *You Hurt Me*[12], when "someone" pulled back to autonomy, the singer responds: "You hurt me . . . just when I thought it was safe to come in. . .you left me like a child in the rain. . you hurt me."

BUT! BUT! BUT!

Being a human means you get to live as a highly developed intellect with the creative freedom and rewards that come with being a person. Making the love in your life last means using that intelligence effectively, because, generally speaking, love can (and often does) override intelligence. Hence the lines exchanged when someone does something very, very foolish in favor of love:

"What the hell were you thinking?"

"I wasn't thinking. I was in love."

ONE MORE "BUT!"

To be a human who can live in pure, true autonomy means at times you *will* feel the loneliness of pure autonomy.[13] And, because the majority of us *do* eventually feel (and dislike) the loneliness of autonomy, we try to stay *away* from it. The draw to love is a very rewarding path away from loneliness, most would agree.[14] *Away from loneliness* puts us in an exciting, natural, and full-of-rewards part of being a human: the *in-love*, *have-sex*, *make-babies*, and the super-exciting *"oh baby oh baby oh baby"* wild abandon of romance part.

---

12 Written by Deborah Allen/Rafe VanHoy/Bobby Braddock, 1998.

13 There is one personality who experiences autonomy without the loneliness. Called "schizoid" for reference sake, these types avoid social activities, seem unable to connect, but they also cope with being alone. "Avoidant" personalities also function in near total autonomy, but it is because *these* individuals find loneliness less severe than the social rejection they find when being social, so they do not interact socially by choice.

14 *"We can cure physical diseases with medicine, but the only cure for loneliness. . . is love."* Agnes Bojaxhiu (Mother Teresa) in *A Simple Path*, 1997.

There are almost seven billion people out there, so the in-love-have-sex-erotic-romance system of making babies *is* effective if all one wants to do is have babies. We seem, however, to have chosen to socialize ourselves away from accepting that our only reason to exist is to make babies. Some might wonder how many births there would be if the process did *not* include the pleasures of sex and love. Random erotic triggers (lust?) *demand* attention. The pleasure available because of the erotic triggers overrides a lot of logical and reasonable thought ("What the hell were you thinking?") because that is exactly what *developmental nature* designed it for. We feel incomplete, lost, lonely, unfulfilled, etc., without romantic love and especially, for some, the *sexual* side of romantic love. We do our best to socialize an accepted *normalcy* into erotic and sexual aspects of romantic love. If we look closely, at times, it appears that *managing the pressures and rewards of erotic sex seems to govern a lot of the major aspects of most societies and cultures*. Look even closer and we realize that society seems to favor one simple guideline regarding socializing acceptable sexual behaviors: Never do anything sexually that you do not want to have appear on the front page of the local newspaper.

No?

Yes! And who *decides* what is acceptable for the local newspapers? Society decides! The society you elect to be a working part of. The society you rely on to provide your rights to separateness and to support your desire to be loved.

WHAT THEN IS THE TRUE HUMAN VALUE OF ROMANTIC LOVE?

There is a thrill available when in love. While the thrill is simply part of the genetic draw to reproduce, we have chosen to socialize it in a very meaningful way that helps us believe we are not simply animals responding to drives, but are capable of overseeing and overriding the drives to bring a humanly beautiful meaning to life.

In this romantic love, the thrill becomes part of everyday existence when two people become aware of what they are truly saying to one another while in love:

Our happiness depends on our meeting one another's need to have good feelings and to not have bad feelings.

Ponder that for a moment. Now, please, <u>ponder it again</u>.

Is it that simple?

Yes, *to have good feelings and to not have bad feelings* is the center point of keeping *any* relationship fulfilling, from the one you have with your grocer to the one you rely on to feel loved. With the grocer, your good feelings come when the food you buy is of quality. The grocer's good feelings come when your check cashes into real money. Simple, then: arrange to have good feelings and not have bad feelings, and *any* relationship succeeds.

In romantic relationships, the basic rule continues: meet my needs by helping me have good feelings and helping me not have bad feelings. The difference is the complexity of the feelings. For instance, consider this truth:

> *My partner's needs, though often very different from my needs, seem every bit as important to them as my needs are to me; and to add to the complexity, needs change.*[15]

Rats! Don't you wish their needs were almost always fully the same as your needs (give or take)?

Well, actually, the needs *do start out the same*. You both say, more or less; "help me feel loved," "hold me, hold me," "please cure my loneliness," "never leave me."

But then, eventually, some inner voice decides that the loneliness is *cured* for the moment. At that time, one of you (the one with the lonely feelings temporarily cured by the shared togetherness) reaches out to reconnect with autonomous separateness. The good feelings you thought you were helping each other have, *changed at that instant* from "hold me hold me," to "give me some space, please." When that change comes *before* one of you is ready to go back to autonomous separateness… it feels like the love might be ending.

---

15 The word "needs" is used to refer to needs, feelings, wants, desires, longings, dreams, etc.

Can you, suddenly, before you actually are ready to, meet the other person's need for space without feeling thrown away? Recall from within and ask yourself: Will he or she come back after getting the requested space? Has he or she come back before? Did this person come back nourished, or come back crabby?

If you cannot meet that *new* good feeling (space) and insist your partner stay close, you just caused a *bad feeling* in him or her (smothered, controlled), something you promised you would help avoid.

Societies appear to continue to insist that true love, once found, will continue to be true. Society (in any of its forms) does not teach the reality we have presented here that *true* love, once found, continues *only* with a mutual understanding to *"please meet my needs by helping me have good feelings and helping me not have bad feelings,"* and then, as long as that reality continues, the feelings of love will continue. Relying on true love to auto-matically nourish itself forever is called *magical thinking.* Santa Claus, tooth fairies, good conquers all, an apple a day keeps the doctor away, are also *magical thinking.*

We've underscored that. Read it again.

Beyond the magic of the initial meeting, the initial look, the initial *knowing*, there is no magic that will continue for long without finding out what feelings he or she finds meaningful, and whether he or she will look to find yours.

True love, once found, continues only with the exchange of promises to "please meet my needs by helping me have good feelings and helping me not have bad feelings." As long as that exchange continues and no one feels compro-mised beyond an acceptable point, the feelings of love will continue.

LET US RESTATE THIS FOR CLARITY

The promises of romantic love are so seductive that for the first time since infanthood it can cause each person to underplay or temporarily forget the importance of the *autonomous* side of their existence. They do not notice that the autonomous identity they've worked on developing for years is quietly being tossed aside in favor of some new rewarding state: the pleasurable dependency of love. Under the umbrella of personal wishes, the statements of love are made. "Please meet my needs by helping me have good feelings and helping me not have bad feelings." If you both define the good feelings as "hold me, hold me, make me feel loved," you then experience a moment when you both get what you want (love). The person giving you love also feels the same feeling (loved). Isn't it grand that at times all you have to do is walk into the room and you make each other's day?

Romantic love focuses almost entirely on the *dependency* (*togetherness*) side of being a person. The being-together part of being in love *initially* overshadows *autonomy* because, by definition, *autonomy* implies aloneness, and too much aloneness becomes loneliness, and because we do not like the lonely state for very long, *autonomy* is often <u>carelessly</u> abandoned for the current loving feelings of *togetherness*.

A couple dated for a year. They've been together every night for months and months. And then:

"Where are you going, Dear?"

"I'm off to play some racquetball tonight."

"But you never play racquetball."

"Oh, yes. In fact, I am the national racquetball champion and must practice at least three nights a week. I've been champ for four years now."

"But, but…why didn't I know that?"

"Huh. I guess I put racquetball aside when I met you. Busy falling in love and all that; the sport seemed trivial then."

"And now? Not so trivial?"

"Oh, no. Not trivial at all, Dear. Racquetball is back with a roar. Anyway, I'm off to practice tonight, and then tomorrow, too. Find something to do, okay?"

Oops!

The fact that *autonomy* does lose some value because of loneliness causes persons in love to ignore that they might, by agreeing to things that seem OKAY at the time, be surrendering vital parts of their autonomous individuality to avoid unwanted loneliness. This will boomerang back sooner, later, or too late.

Witness conversations such as:

(1) "How long are you going to be gone?" (The feelings behind this question often are: "I can feel lost when you leave—please hurry back." But the feelings can also be: "I need some time to myself also.")

(2) "I'll work on this now if you help me on it after a while." (The feelings? "I want the freedom to work alone on this, but I'm afraid if I ignore you for long you'll leave me, so I'll *pretend* I want your opinions later.")

(3) "As long as I get enough sex, you can run the rest of my life." (Feelings? "Erotic triggers rule me, and I like that I can turn to you whenever I want sex.")

The values of *autonomy* (freedom, expression, self-identity, choices, etc.) slide into the background in favor of the more immediate pleasure offered by the opposite of loneliness: the *togetherness*, the love. Remember also, as a plus, romantic love is accompanied by the promise and availability of the erotic fulfillment of sex with a partner. In our autonomous state, to be erotic offers only sex with self and usually does not deliver what sex with a partner promises.[16]

So, when lonely, we *run* to the heavy presence and glory of the romantic relationship. The true *autonomy* of each "you" in the relationship is voluntarily abandoned (bye-bye, racquetball) leaving only the romantic *togetherness* sides of each of you. So, the tricky part of love is revealed now. It is not just "hold me, hold me, make me happy." That is easy. The tricky part is unsaid and pops up later when one of you wants some autonomy back. The truthful love statement should not have been "hold me, hold me, make me feel loved." It is rightfully: "Please hold me, hold me, and let me feel loved until I want to go back to feeling some autonomy, *okay?*"

Why didn't they make that clearer?

Love is challenged and can be in danger (unconsciously pushed aside) when the very first draw for autonomy begins to tap one of you for attention. No matter how wonderful the romantic love is, autonomy will creep back in. People will fight the return of autonomy for fear it is a signal that if love is set aside, it might not return.

Place yourself on both sides of trying to understand and accept this vital dividing point of a couple's autonomy/togetherness adventure. You are holding, loving and kissing and expect to be there for several more hours for more of the same. You assume he/she is on the same holding, loving and kissing page. Instead, suddenly, he/she slips away from your arms.

---

16 Sex with self: see "five types of sex" in *Men & Sex, Heroes & Jerks*, Huntington, Vince. Cutler Publishing, La Jolla, CA, 2000.

"I have to telephone my sister now and finalize some details on Saturday's family reunion. This'll take the rest of the evening."

Duhh!

You might immediately feel disappointed, confused, pushed away, rejected; tricked by life. If you wish to save the relationship and eventually return to the loving togetherness place, your J.O.B. is to accept his/her shift to autonomy and not let the unintended rejection become the focus of the relationship. Your rejected feeling is REAL, but has no REAL value other than you just learned that he/she is not very good at shifting from togetherness to autonomy within a relationship. The future quality of the relationship will be defined by how well you two manage this shift and to establish how far in advance any future announcements of the needs for autonomy are to be; "no surprises, please."

If after she/he returns from family reunion prepping (or any autonomous task), does he/she return fulfilled and nourished, or come back crabby? If he/she returns fulfilled and ready for closeness again, autonomy/togetherness balance is in pretty good order. If returning crabby and distracted, the balance is out of balance. On the other side of this happening, you are holding and being held. Ahh love divine. Soon however, you become distracted by thoughts of a letter you have to have ready for the boss by tomorrow. The autonomous side of you just stepped in ahead of the togetherness side even though a few micro-seconds before the distracting letter duty took shape, holding and loving was very very nice; togetherness had ruled everything.

NO MAN IS AN ISLAND—ANY PORT IN A STORM

From early in life, we appear to balance between being taken care of, with its eventual smothering feeling, and being a separate person, with its eventual accompanying fear of loneliness. We go out, come back, have fun, become fearful, get close, too close, run out again…on and on as though throughout life we want to believe someone is always going to be there to catch us, or is always watching our back, but is never out to truly mis-use us, smother us, or kill off our autonomy. When we find signs of that all balanced in our arms, we call it love.

Think back: as a child you wanted a parent to watch you swim, but not to stop you to tell you *how*. Well, maybe some days you did.

REVIEW TIME

You now know: too much autonomy becomes loneliness and romantic love distracts from loneliness...but *too much* roman-tic love feels smothering and might threaten autonomy...and being alone relieves the smothering...so there will be swings from one to the other and back throughout your life, sometimes daily, even hourly, or even moment to moment. Yes, each sec-ond for some, so recognize and manage it.

Some examples:
    (1) Off to the ball game to be alone and just kick back. All is perfect well into the fifth or sixth inning, when your team bursts way into the lead. You sort of wish *she* were there to share the fun; after all, it is her favorite team, too. You suddenly wonder why you hadn't invited her.

(2) "Ahh, he's gone for the day. Good. I can read that book I've been saving for these quiet moments." Later, book finished, day becoming evening, the house begins to feel empty. "Where *is* that guy now? How I do miss him."

(3) "I want her to go to the movie with me. I also want her to like it. What if she doesn't like it? How much difference (autonomy) can I be okay with? Why do I need her to like the same movie? She has her own mind about which movies she likes. She is real autonomous there. I am sure dependent there. I actually want someone in my life who agrees with whatever I believe is a good movie. Wow! Says a lot about me."

AND THE POINT IS?

Our happiness depends on our meeting one another's needs to have good feelings and to not have bad feelings.

Our *job* is to remember we are being asked to meet others' needs[17] by helping them have certain good feelings and by helping them

---

17 And remember the word "needs" is used to refer to needs, feelings, wants, desires, longings, dreams, etc

not have certain bad feelings. We are asking the same from them…good feelings, please, no bad feelings, thank you.

When the feelings we both wanted were mutual—make me feel loved—we were lucky we both needed the same thing at the same time. Now, however, that need is not to *always* need romantic love to dominate. We want to trust that now I can go out and be me, and come back for the love. We also have to develop and support a willingness to accept that our partner wants the same thing at times. Now, the balancing of your separateness and togetherness with his or her separateness and togetherness becomes the good or bad feelings to be honored or avoided.

Practice! It is a skill you two are working on.

A skill?

Yes, it is a skill, because needs will change. Remember from earlier:

My partner's needs, though often very different from my needs, seem every bit as important to him or her as my needs are to me. Besides that, needs will change.

Well, even though needs might change, you still have promised one another you will help each other have good feelings and not have bad feelings. Feelings change, as needs do, so establish some way to routinely keep up with one another's needs and changes. It is truly a skill reflecting how well you communicate details of the needs and feelings.[18]

And note this: Often we are not even aware we have a certain need of our own *until it is not met*. For instance, say you go into a new restaurant for lunch and sit down to order. You suddenly become aware the place is not right. It is not what you had in mind. In fact, it is so far from what you needed that you get up and leave without a word. That is a perfect example of not knowing you had a certain need for a certain ambience *until it was not met*.

18 Communication as a skill is examined and particularized in detail in Part IV of *A Journal for All Relationships.*

In another example, you go to dinner with a new date and he or she orders a third drink before the meal comes. You suddenly feel disappointed, sort of empty and trapped. You had not accounted for how important it was for your date to not be a heavy drinker…until it became obvious that need was not being met.

We do not manage knowing all of our needs all of the time. An unnoticed need will often surprise you. Sometimes we get so busy being one aspect of our self that we do not even notice what we *really* want at the moment is some other aspect of our self.

Just recognize and accept that the perfect set of scales between the <u>separate us</u> and the <u>together us</u> is never permanent but is ever in motion. Even when life presents the best of both available worlds—to be loved and yet still be a recognizable separate personality—our needs will change as they are met or unmet. We have romantic love offering one set of changing needs, and we have a separate self-identity forever expressing itself with changing needs (but one where we like to feel we are loved even though separate). Cater to them both, but be aware: your lover will have the same need to balance his or her own sense of those differences. By the way, neither of you will have identical needs for balance; one almost always feels a little crowded, the other feels a little pushed away.

WHAT ABOUT THE GROCER?

We did promise that this information would improve and maintain romantic relationships but would also be good for any relationship, including your relationship with your grocer or the person you buy gasoline from weekly. With very little imagination, you can see how the balance applies and how the grocer's changing needs might also bounce off of your expectations. The grocer might press you to buy his avocados one day because he needs some quick income, and you *might* feel some pressure to please him. But, because you do not rely on him for 80 to 90 percent of your daily happiness, it will be easier to just say no to his avocados than it would be to say no to a spouse's *need* to have a nice dinner out, or clean out the garage, or entertain a crabby in-law for two weeks.

"No, Mr. Grocer Person, I have no need for avocados today. Thanks." The grocer will move on to someone else to meet his need to sell the avocados.

However, if you say, "No, Spouse Person, I have no need to please you today. Thanks," that spouse person may then also move on to someone else to meet the need for dinner out, the clean garage, or his or her parent to visit.

Feel a little out of balance with the spouse?

WHAT ABOUT TIT FOR TAT?

It sure seems as though tit for tat (equivalent retaliation) should work interpersonally, but it does not.

"I wish you would wipe off the counter better after you make a sandwich."

"Why? You never wipe the bathroom sink clean after you use it."

"Oh!"

Did they trade meaningfully there?

When we try to trade things to pretend we are meeting a certain need (to wipe off the counter better) both the original need (please wipe off the counter) and the one we try trading go unmet. If there is a need to have your partner "clean the bathroom sink better," that is a separate subject from the need to "wipe off the counter better after you make a sandwich."

"Oh, you want me to wipe the counter better? I'll do my best."

Followed by:

"That reminds me. When you use the bathroom sink, would you rinse it out? I hate stopping my morning shower-shave rush to clean that sink."

"Oh! Okay, I'll do my best there."

When we make a promise to meet a need, we *genuinely* mean to follow through. If we neglect to, it is usually simply because we became real busy being us...that separate us, that *autonomous* us.

AS GOOD AS IT GETS

In 1997 there was an Oscar-winning movie, *As Good As It Gets,* defining this point.[19] The point of the movie was that perhaps as we reach for ultimate 24-7 happiness, we forget that it is an *average fulfillment* that *truly* registers overall quality. Some might call that *compromise,* but that word has been used too long to mean *loss* or *doing without,* etc. See it as an agreement: "I'll go your way for now, knowing that we will go *my* way another day on another subject or need."

We now offer a new idea. Step back and seriously watch yourself change daily, from an autonomous you to *dependency*, hour by hour; you *alone* vs. you *two*, even moment by moment, alone, riding the waves by yourself with the wind in your hair vs. holding someone close, on the same waves, in the same wind.

---

19 *As Good As It Gets,* 1997, Tri-Star, Oscar-winning movie with Jack Nicholson and Helen Hunt.

SMOTHERED-TOGETHERNESS-ROMANCE-BALANCED-FULFILLED-AUTONOMY-LONELY

⌐------------------------*Feeling Loved*------------⌐

WATCH OUT...A TRAP, A TRICK

There is another built-in human weakness in maintaining the desired symmetry. We have a tendency to run away too quickly from *any* undesired experiences (bad feelings) of *either* farthest end of separateness or togetherness. If we are not careful, we will be continually running from the one extreme to the other every moment, every day. From loneliness (when too autonomous), we will run to the rescuing pleasure of feeling *loved* which can *actually*, eventually, become smothering.

You might then find yourself going back and forth at full speed, full time, over and over, smothering, to freedom to loneliness and back to smothering. We again tend to run far away from feeling smothered. We drive off to the resort, alone, perhaps with a good book. The first period of time in that place, alone, would likely feel great, feel free, of course. But, you see already? After four or five hours (days, weeks), the extreme of autonomy brings back the loneliness that took you to the smothering in the first place.

Running from or trying to avoid one extreme or the other can be confusing to initially sort out. For example:

"Hold me, but not too tightly."

"I'm going for a walk by myself" (and, later, to complain) "Why didn't you call me on my cell while I was walking?"

"Please go see your friends, but not *all* friends, and don't be gone *all* evening."

"I want to go shopping with my friends but I'm afraid you'll be mad at me if I leave you alone."

"If you love me, set me free" the smothered voice speaks in contradiction.

Never run in panic from *either* extreme. You'll overshoot the balance point and just have to come back. Instead, consciously wander out, look around, and then calmly assess and then describe your feelings and needs.

A major step in applying this skill in a relationship is to be able to openly tell your lover when either loneliness or smothering begins to rule you.

"I want some time to myself soon, but I'm afraid you'll feel rejected."

"I won't if the time is reasonable." (Who defines "reasonable"?)

"When I am working on my own project, I feel like you feel neglected. It makes it hard for me to concentrate and enjoy my project."

"I really do not mind when you work on your project. You seem to get nourished by it, so I benefit eventually."

"I guess I need some continuous magic sign that when I am busy being me, you are okay with it."

"I'll speak up. I promise."

"With plenty of warning time?" (Who defines "plenty"?)

"Of course. Please do not worry that I'll want to give you away because you have a project to work on. I often have my own projects."

"It helps talking about it."

AND DO NOT FORGET, NEEDS WILL CHANGE

"I liked it when we went to the movies on Friday evenings after work."

"I don't want to go after work anymore. I'm too tired to enjoy them."

"Oh!"

Or

"I don't like it when you drink so much you get giddy."

"You used to think I was cute when I drank."

"That was then. It's not cute now."

"Oh!"

Needs *do* change.[20]

THE DESIRABLE IDEAL

Once aware of this balancing act, equal balance *is* a logical, desirable ideal. It contains the better of the two aspects of being human. Practice recognizing your own balance, which, in *autonomy*, includes everything from refreshing alone time and creative expression, to being foolish and carefree, seeing faces in the clouds, daydreaming about that electrifying *something* you are going to do some day...just busy being *you*.

In *dependency*, it includes the *pleasure and acceptance* of loving and being loved, of smiling at your partner, of causing them to smile, feeling adored, being held, holding on so they feel cared for, touching, laying back, daydreaming about that *other* wonderful something you two will do together some day. At the moment, they *are* the *other you*.

---

20 While romantic love is used above to explain the dependency chunk, dependency also includes everyday social acceptance, a place to work, to play, to feel cared for and safe in a community.

TRUE LOVE AND SELFISHNESS[21]

There's a strong social ideal that being matched in love is what life is all about, but that being caught up in one's self (separateness) is sometimes seen as self-centered or *selfish*. Anyone who is selfish is seen as shallow, overly self-absorbed. Confusing phrases like "it's all about you" and "selfish people *use* others" are thrown about carelessly.[17]

That idea is distorted and plainly not true. Humans *cannot* stop self-identifying. We can't stop being us. Try it and see. Go on. Try to *not* be you.

Did you do it?

Oh yeah?

---

21 "Selfish" is a term devised by parents and some others to keep control of you; it truly gives control to the one using the word. We humans are self-invested, yes. If we were not, who would actually take care of the details of our life? We are busy being "us" most of the time. Be careful of someone who calls you selfish. "*Unselfish,*" a six-year old girl once told me, "means you get your toy back broken."

Instead of making us all "wrong" for being self-invested, let's just accept it, encourage it, and fold it into the omelet of truth along with the fact that we're all trying to maintain a balance of our autonomy and dependency. Besides, if you didn't concentrate on your own best interests, who would? Well, actually, many in your society will volunteer to tell you what your best interests are, but can they really speak for you, the individual you?

Society as a whole likes to promote good order and togetherness, and, while a sense of order is a good thing, social forces seem to habitually obtain their desired order by squelching a lot of individuality and autonomy. Most of us feel pressure to fit in at various times in our lives.

Society (remember, that is whomever we chose to be with) often decrees extremes of individuality as anti-social, unwanted, troubling, or selfish. Be careful there. Identify your autonomy and follow it. Someone will go with you.

By chasing someone else's idealized *together life,* you may end up smothered by social pressures, trapped in an unfulfilling job, powerless to quit the job because you *must* pay for an overpriced apartment because you have two kids born accidentally too early into your life, and you have an equally smothered spouse, and the two of you have a lot of *bad feelings*, not too many *good feelings*, and no one to blame except yourselves. *Honor your autonomy.* The human need to *eventually* love and be loved is not a bad thing at all. It is, however, a thing to be realistically timed and measured, recognized and honored. As one woman said a month into married life:

"Wow, this togetherness business is here, 24 friggin' 7." The same applies to needs for autonomy. It, too, is a real thing that needs measured, recognized, and honored.

"It was great to leave that marriage and be free again, but that was a year ago. Wow! Now, I'm lonely, but every available person out there has at least two kids and an ex. Feels like if I connect up again to make my loneliness go away I'll only end up feeling smothered again, this time by someone *else's* kids. Maybe if I had learned how to not be so smothered when married, I'd still have the good parts of my old life."

And here it is, all restated in a nutshell.

With the passing of time, <u>even a time of wonderful togetherness</u>, *one of you* will eventually feel the first sign of the need to step away from the togetherness. It will perhaps be a simple sense of being ever-so-slightly out of sorts, feeling pestered or annoyed. You will likely try and try again to return to the wonderfulness of love you were experiencing a few seconds ago. You might even expect the other person to bring back the wonderfulness. After all, he or she "caused" the wonderfulness in the first place, right? You will both likely become confused. Either way, autonomy will pull at you, but it does *not* mean you must run as far and as fast as the thirst for autonomy will try to take you. Slow down! Wait! Listen! Feel the balance return. See how long it takes. Learn from it. Tell one another what it is like.

REVIEW OF THE REVIEW

Why in one microsecond can *togetherness* be so fulfilling and then, suddenly, it is so smothering? While *autonomy* cancels the smothering feeling, it will at first feel wonderful and free and so, so right, but eventually (slowly, or in some cases suddenly) a jolt of loneliness appears, and that feeling of missing the love-togetherness-dependency connection we had fled from not long ago, whether it has been three minutes or three weeks or three months.

One person said it well several years ago when speaking to friends about his newfound love:

"I left the bed and walked to the window overlooking the bay, where I looked out into the night. I had a breathtaking feeling of complete happiness, but yet, at the same time, a need to stay away from the bed. I asked myself, 'Why the need to be away from that closeness when one moment ago the entire world seemed centered on my being close to her?' "

Have we answered that person's question?

A Simple Test:

Ask yourself, "Can I be in a relationship with *that* person and not lose who I am?"

DO WE FALL OUT OF LOVE?

Separateness and togetherness be damned, we are here to make babies.[22] Living a purely sex-drive-driven life to just make babies may have been all right in earlier stages of our development as human beings; however, balancing the pleasures and drives to make babies with the equal pleasure and the developing drives to be an individual separate from baby-making results in life a lot different from how it was originally intended by nature. *We are humans.* We *truly* do suffer when we experience a loss or even the threat of a loss of autonomous identity, _and_

---

22 Religious posturing aside, it is our animal drive to procreate (God given or evolved) that draws us to romantic love, the drive to procreate being the cause of loneliness and its cure.

we *also* suffer from an absence of love. We often suffer both at once and each because of the other. And…we still like to have babies at times.

Men and women alike *appear* to forget how influential and ever present the overall human mission to procreate is. It takes many forms to accomplish its genetically programmed mission. Socially integrated into our lives in an almost conniving way, the very complex sets of rules regarding love, sex, babies, family, heirs, villages, and cultures cause many to go through life believing they are their own autonomous person only to discover (often too late) they have somehow become a servant of the basic human mission—they are raising babies at the loss of their own sense of self, of his or her autonomy *separate* from doing the baby raising.

"Boo-hiss," many will say to this theme that somehow we are practically slaves to the basic drive to procreate. Their boo-hissing testifies to how those boo-hissing individuals might be so over influenced, even tricked, by the drives for which they actually act as agents.

In the example of the man by the window, the question could come up—am I falling out of love?

Surely, the person in the bed might feel rejected by being left alone. He or she might wonder if his or her lover has suddenly fallen out of love. Or, in as many cases, they are enjoying the peace of being alone, regrouping, perhaps digesting being loved.

We do not *fall out of love*. We simply misidentify the natural shifts that take place between the epitome of one or the other extremes of this wonder of human existence. After making love, needs changed with the couple in the bed. Need for autonomy returned to one, whereas the need to reflect in the lovemaking continued for the other. "Help me have good feelings and help me not have bad feelings" remains the center of the love. It is just that the feelings needed are forever shifting.

Learn the shifts of that person who brought you love to share.

Now please, go forth and love.

Vince and Sally Huntington are psychotherapists licensed as marriage and family therapists. They first met in graduate school, where they discovered through internships that together they had a knack for assessing what was really taking place in unhappy marriages and, over time, were able to apply what they saw to *any* human relationship.

Vince and Sally hosted a radio show in San Diego for ten years where they were able to empirically test and formally research their observations of what defines a fulfilling relationship.

Over the years, they've identified six critical areas that must be well understood and consciously catered to for a relationship to continue to be satisfying and supportive. Relationships no longer nourish when:

(1) Basic *trust* is taken for granted but *never actually defined*.
(2) Communication fails (she or he just does not hear you) and anger begins to rule.
(3) Family presence obstructs the lifestyle of the relationship (parent pressures, ill child, siblings, stepparents, etc.).
(4) Money styles clash (savers marry spenders).
(5) Sex and affection are misunderstood, out of sync, or out of control.
6) When the couple forgets that they are individuals and can unconsciously and unwillingly lose their individuality to the marriage.

The Balancing Act is Part I of *A Journal for All Relationships* by Vince and Sally Huntington, © January 2011. They invite you to count on these books to provide objective insight to *your* present or future marriage and to begin to apply these skills to *any* relationship, yes, even to that person from whom you buy your groceries.

Appendix I

Two simple tests to check your current balance of autonomy and dependency in whatever relationships you use to compare (marriage, parenting, employer/employee, even grocer).

Test 1.
The Three Famous *Marriage Whisperer Questions.*

(1) If you did not know (fill in name) would you be looking for (that person), to be in your life just as they are, as you truly know them? Yes ____ No ____

(2) If (fill in name) said he or she no longer wanted to be part of you life, what is your FIRST feeling?

_____

(3) If (fill in name) truly was out of my life, what could I, would I be able to do different each day that I can not or do not do because he/she is in my life?

_____

Test 2.
Balance Measurement

Test your relationships. (Not all questions will fit all relationships)

1. When your partner is autonomous (does their own thing) does she/he come back nourished, fulfilled, smiling? I.E: (Does your golfer (or 'shopper') come back happy?)
1 – never, 2- hardly ever, 3- now and again, 4- most always, 5- always. ____ ____

2. When *you* are autonomous (do your own thing) for some time and some reason, are you 'welcomed back'? (Do you get open arms?)
1 – never, 2- hardly ever, 3- now and again, 4- most always, 5- always. ____ ____

3. Does your partner tell you early enough before he/she does his/her own thing, to where you don't feel surprised, left out or abandoned?
1 – never, 2- hardly ever, 3- now and again, 4- most always, 5- always. ____ ____

4. Does your partner accept that your autonomy (alone time) is important to you - and actually help you get it?

1 – never, 2- hardly ever, 3- 50-50, 4- most always, 5- always. ____ ____

5. How many of your partner's autonomous nourishing pastimes can you name?

1- none really, 2- not sure, 3- one or two, 4- several, 5- all of them. ____ ____

6. Is it easy for you two to schedule time together?

1 – never, 2- hardly ever, 3- now and again, 4- most always, 5- always. ____ ____

7. Do you get 'enough' time together?

1 – never, 2- hardly ever, 3- now and again, 4- most always, 5- always. ____ ____

8. When together, overall, do you feel:

1 - smothered, 2 - controlled, 3 - okay, 4 - pretty nice, 5 – loved? ____ ____

9. Can you sense when your behaviors about being alone or needing closeness are near the acceptable limits of your relationship?

1- not ever, 2, hardly ever, 3- so-so, 4, almost always, 5 – always? ____ ____

10. Does your partner seem to take for granted that you will always quickly adjust to his/her separate or togetherness times?

1- most always, 2 –often, 3 – not noticeable, 4 – seldom, 5 never. ____ ____

11. Can you count on him/her accepting it when you 'get too busy to fulfill a promise'?

1- not ever, 2, hardly ever, 3- so-so, 4, almost always, 5 – always? ____ ____

12. How much has your partner's autonomy cause you to feel shut-out?

1- nearly always, 2- a lot, 3 – so-so, 4, hardly ever, 5, not ever. ____ ____

13. Do your partner's autonomous goings-on help you to be more autonomous in a favorable way.

1 - no, 2- some, 3- so-so, 4- yes, 5- very much. ____ ____

14. Do your partner's autonomous goings-on embarrass you?

1- constantly, 2- often, 3- now and again, 4- very seldom. 5 – never. ____ ____

15. When with your partner, do you feel better about yourself?
1- never, 2 hardly ever, 3 - at times, 4 - often, 5 - nearly always. ____ ____

16. Do your partner's autonomous goings-on improve your perspective on life?
1 – never, 2 – not clear if it does, 3- some, 4 – considerably, 5 - always. ____ ____

17. Do you do autonomous 'things' in order to coax your partner to be more involved in life?
1, – often, 2 – of course, 3 - some times, 4 - not consciously, 5 – never. ____ ____

18. Do you count on your partner to approve of _your_ autonomy?
1- yes, 2, perhaps at times, 3 – not sure, 4 - not consciously, 5 – never. ____ ____

19. Do you actually _feel_ loved?
1 – not really, 2 – some times, 3 usually, 4 – mostly, 5 – always. ____ ____

20. Are you disappointed at how much alone time he/she takes?
1 – always, 2 – most always 3 - at times, 4 – hardly ever, 5- never. ____ ____

21. When very _busy being you_, do you still feel your romance is alive?
1 – never, 2 – hardly ever, 3 – usually, 4 – almost always, 5 – yes. ____ ____

22. If you find yourself feeling left out when he/she is _busy being them_, do you convert it to being 'glad' he/she is enjoying their life?
1. never, 2 – can't picture that, 3 – hardly ever, 4 - now and again, 5 – often ____ ____.

23. Of 100 percent of your life, what percentage are you being "you" either autonomously or dependently ?
1- less than 10%, 2 -20 to 40%, 3 – 40 to 60%, 4 – 60 to 80%, 5 – over 90%. ____ ____

24. Are your autonomy needs balanced with your dependency needs?
1 – never, 2 – hardly ever, 3 – so-so, 4- almost always, 5 – near perfectly. ____ ____

25. Do you believe your partner requires you to ignore your autonomy?
1. almost always, 2- quite often, 3 – if I let it, 4 – not really, 5- never. ____ ____

26. Do you believe your partner requires you to ignore your dependency (togetherness) needs?
1. almost always, 2- quite often, 3 – if I let it, 4 – not really, 5- never. ____ ____

27. Does his or her dependency needs dominate your relationship?
1. almost always, 2- quite often, 3 – if I let it, 4 – not really, 5- never. ____ ____

28. Does his or her autonomous needs dominate your relationship?
1. almost always, 2- quite often, 3 – if I let it, 4 – not really, 5- never. ____ ____

29. Does your combined 'lifestyle' not counting your partner, keep you from being 'you'?
1- most always, 2- pretty often, 3- at times, 4- hardly ever, 5- most never. ____ ____

30. Does your 'family' (however you define family, not counting your partner) Expect you to be the same as you were when at home as a child?
1- most always, 2- pretty often, 3- at times, 4- hardly ever, 5- most never.
____ ____

Total score
130 to150 Very Balanced Relationship. Nicely Done
115 to130 A Little Work To Do.
 75 to115 A Lot Of Work To Do
        Below 75 Someone, Maybe Both, are
        Very Compromised.
        Suggest re-read pages 10-16

Index

Reviews May 2011

The Huntington's help light the tricky pathways for anyone in ANY relationship. Short and to the point, *The Balancing Act* works. Larry Corrigan, marriage and Family Therapist and Licensed Social Worker, San Diego, Ca.

The Balancing Act makes it so very clear. – balancing togetherness and separateness is the key to rewarding couple relationships. Leah Kramer, LMFT. Military couples specialist. San Diego, Ca.

An illustrated, fun to read 36 pages, *The Balancing Act* combines practical advice with highly interesting examples to supplement and clarify the basic principles of relationships of any kind. There is enough power in these pages to light many lamps. John Cotter. B Sc., MBA, FBIET. President, John J. Cotter & Assoc Inc. La Jolla Ca.

The Huntington's provide a sensible and straightforward method for transforming one's emotional life and one's relationships. The level of communication in the world would elevate dramatically if everyone learned their approach. A. Tom Horvath, Ph.D., ABPP, President, Practical Recovery.

The Balancing Act is brilliant and incisive writing and certainly applies to a much wider readership than just "couples". An excellent coverage of life. Mariam Alexanian Duckwall. Ardent reader & Professor of Theatre Arts, Michigan State (ret).

Short and to the point, with no nonsense and no psychobabble; *The Balancing Act* by Vince and Sally Huntington make complex relationship issues so very clear. A must read for therapists *and* couples. Sandra Gorchow Licensed Marriage Therapist, La Jolla, Ca.

Made in the USA
San Bernardino, CA
20 November 2017